The Real Story Behind Clarkson's Farm

A British Farming Revolution

Arshey Ashveil

Copyright

Disclaimer

This book is an independent, journalistic exploration of the themes, realities, and public impact of the television series Clarkson's Farm and the broader state of British agriculture. It is **not affiliated with, endorsed by, or officially connected to Jeremy Clarkson, Amazon Prime Video, or any individuals or production entities associated with the show**.

All references to Clarkson's Farm, its cast, and related public commentary are drawn from publicly available sources and are used for **educational, analytical, and commentary purposes** under fair use principles.

While every effort has been made to ensure the accuracy of information at the time of writing, **facts, policies, and statistics may** *evolve*, and readers are encouraged to consult official sources such as DEFRA, the NFU, and local farming organizations for the most current data.

The views expressed in this book are those of the author and contributing analysts and do not necessarily reflect the views of the individuals or entities mentioned herein.

This work is intended for **informative and educational purposes only**.

Table of Contents

Introduction

Few expected that a man known for racing cars, insulting French people, and mocking vegetarians would become the most unlikely ambassador for British farming. But when *Clarkson's Farm* hit Amazon Prime in 2021, it didn't just entertain—it struck a national nerve. What started as a celebrity vanity project turned into a phenomenon that made millions laugh, think, and for the first time in years, truly notice the people who grow our food.

Jeremy Clarkson had owned land in the Cotswolds for years. But when his farm manager retired, he made a decision as impulsive as it was sincere—he would take over the job himself. No experience. No training. Just one man, a giant Lamborghini tractor, and a film crew. It could've been a disaster. Instead, it became one of the most talked-about documentaries in Britain, and perhaps the most honest portrayal of rural life the country had ever seen on screen.

At its heart, the show was funny. Clarkson stumbling through muddy fields, losing sheep, crashing equipment, and getting scolded by young, sharp-tongued Kaleb Cooper became instant classics. But behind the humor, something deeper resonated. Clarkson wasn't just clowning around—he was discovering, in real time, just how complicated, exhausting, and unforgiving farming really is. And so were we.

The timing couldn't have been more perfect—or more dire. Britain was reeling from the aftershocks of Brexit. Farmers were facing lost subsidies, labor shortages, export headaches, and a mountain of new paperwork. At the same time, COVID-19 had exposed the fragility of supply chains. Supermarket shelves were thinning, and for the first time in a generation, people were asking questions like: Who actually grows our food? Where does it come from? What if they stop?

Clarkson's Farm showed us those answers. It showed us that farming wasn't just tractors and cows. It was forms, weather apps, crushed budgets, and moments of bitter defeat. It was watching a year's worth of work vanish in a week of bad rain. It was being told by a council officer that you couldn't sell potatoes without jumping through legal hoops. It was about dealing with rules made by people who'd never set foot in a field.

Audiences didn't just watch. They connected. Urban viewers who'd never seen a sheep in real life found themselves rooting for Clarkson's livestock. People who never cared about crop rotation suddenly found wheat fascinating. Characters like Kaleb and Gerald—authentic, unpolished, and deeply competent—became surprise stars. Kaleb, a young man with no intention of ever setting foot in London, captured hearts with his work ethic and refusal to let Clarkson's fame get in the way of doing the job right.

The media noticed too. Headlines rolled in. Articles debated the show's accuracy, praised its honesty, and criticized its bureaucracy. Politicians even began referencing it in Parliament. The National Farmers' Union called it one of the most powerful portrayals of modern farming ever broadcast. Clarkson, once mocked for his brashness, had managed to humanize a profession often stereotyped and ignored.

What made it work wasn't that it was perfect. It was that it was messy. Real. Clarkson made mistakes—big ones—and he didn't hide them. He didn't pretend to be an expert. Instead, he learned in front of us, asked stupid questions, got things wrong, and most importantly, *listened*. And through his journey, we listened too.

Farming became dinner table talk. Kids began asking their parents about tractors. Farmers, long unseen, were finally being seen. The show planted something no one expected: empathy. For the first time in years, the British public looked past the rolling hills and picturesque landscapes and saw the sweat, frustration, and pride beneath it all.

This book isn't about Jeremy Clarkson the TV host. It's about what *Clarkson's Farm* revealed—the truth behind the jokes. The policies, the economics, the lives entangled in our fields. It's about a country waking up to how broken and brilliant its agricultural system can be. And it's about the people who've been carrying that weight quietly for generations.

Because whether you're tuning in for the comedy or staying for the cows, one thing is now impossible to deny: Farming has never mattered more—and finally, someone put it in the spotlight.

Chapter One

Jeremy Clarkson – From Top Gear to Tractor Tires

When Jeremy Clarkson announced he was trading supercars for sheep, many assumed it was a joke—or at best, a stunt. After all, this was the man who had spent decades roaring down racetracks, mocking cyclists, and declaring that the only soil he respected was the tarmac of a Formula 1 circuit. Farming, to most of his fans, felt wildly out of character. But as the world would soon find out, the leap from gearboxes to grain wasn't just genuine—it was transformative.

The truth is, Clarkson had quietly owned a farm in Oxfordshire for years. It wasn't a whimsical purchase; it came as part of a larger estate he bought in 2008. For a long time, he left the actual farming to a professional manager, like many landowners do. But in 2019, when that manager retired, Clarkson made a decision that would change his life—and, unknowingly, the national conversation around agriculture. Instead of hiring a replacement, he decided to do it himself. "How hard could it be?" he quipped. Famous last words.

The move was met with the kind of collective eye-roll the British public reserves for celebrities dabbling in the real world.

Critics were skeptical. Commentators called it a vanity project. Farmers—many of whom had spent their lives battling real hardship—braced for a shallow portrayal. Social media lit up with sarcasm. Clarkson? Farming? Surely this was a setup for another punchline.

But then the cameras rolled, and what emerged surprised almost everyone.

Clarkson, despite his larger-than-life personality, didn't try to fake competence. In fact, he leaned into his ignorance. From the moment he climbed aboard an absurdly large Lamborghini tractor (which he later admitted was completely impractical), viewers saw a man utterly out of his depth—and willing to admit it. He wasn't pretending to be a farmer. He was trying to become one. And every mistake, every muddied boot, every baffled conversation with local experts showed that transformation in real time.

There was something deeply symbolic in that struggle. Here was one of the most recognizable figures in British entertainment—a millionaire, an icon, a man used to being the smartest in the room—reduced to standing in the rain, staring helplessly at a broken gate or a flooded field. It wasn't just good television. It was, perhaps unintentionally, a statement about humility.

Clarkson's learning curve was steep. He wrestled with the basics: crop rotation, lambing season, fertilizer schedules, the maddening unpredictability of British weather. He grappled with DEFRA paperwork that made even seasoned farmers groan. He made expensive errors. He tried, failed, tried again. And crucially, he listened—to Kaleb Cooper, his young but sharp farmhand; to Gerald, his soft-spoken stone wall expert; and to Lisa Hogan, his partner and sounding board. The dynamic was clear: fame didn't matter here. Nature didn't care who he was. Neither did the sheep.

It was this willingness to fail publicly that won people over. Viewers expected comedy—and got it—but what they didn't expect was vulnerability. Clarkson began to speak with reverence about the land, about the exhaustion of farm work, about the endless financial risks. He openly admitted that he'd never appreciated farmers before. He wasn't preaching—he was confessing.

The reaction from the farming community, initially wary, began to shift. While some remained critical—concerned the show might oversimplify or exaggerate—many saw value in the exposure. Finally, someone with a platform was highlighting the insanity of certain regulations, the emotional toll of bad harvests, the disconnect between supermarket shoppers and the soil. Clarkson, for all his rough edges, was giving farmers something they hadn't had in years: visibility.

Outside the agricultural world, his new role became a point of national intrigue. In pubs, offices, and online forums, people discussed field yields, lambing stress, and tractor types. It was as if Britain had remembered that it was, at its roots, a country built on farming. And the man who reminded them was someone who, only months earlier, had been test-driving a Bugatti.

The symbolism of Clarkson's journey goes even deeper. In a world obsessed with celebrity success and curated perfection, here was a man showing real failure, real fatigue, and real growth. He wasn't saving the farming industry single-handedly—but he was *trying*. And that act of trying, of entering a field he knew nothing about, of shedding ego in favor of effort, struck a chord far beyond the Cotswolds.

Jeremy Clarkson, the loudest man in Britain, had stumbled into one of the quietest, hardest, most essential jobs in the country. And in doing so, he reminded the nation that there is dignity in dirt, nobility in labor, and grace in learning something the hard way.

Chapter Two

Diddly Squat – The Anatomy of a Real British Farm

From a distance, Clarkson's farm looks like something out of a countryside postcard. Gently rolling hills, fields stretching into the horizon, clusters of hedgerows and stone fences baked in golden light. But anyone who has ever tried to manage such land knows: it's not a landscape, it's a living thing—and it rarely behaves.

Nestled in the Cotswolds, Jeremy Clarkson's **Diddly Squat Farm** spans around **1,000 acres** of arable land near **Chadlington**, a quiet Oxfordshire village. The region is known for its postcard charm and wealthy retirees, not necessarily for cutting-edge agriculture. Yet beneath its bucolic beauty lies a land with quirks, demands, and personality.

The name "Diddly Squat" might sound like a joke—and it is. But it also reflects a hard truth: despite the size of the property, Clarkson's earnings from actual farming efforts amounted to next to nothing in his first year. "Diddly squat" is slang for *almost nothing*—and in this case, it was a very literal financial summary. In that, Clarkson joined a long and painful tradition of UK smallholders scraping by on narrow margins.

The farm's terrain is typical of **South East England's limestone uplands**—good for some arable crops but not without its limitations. The **soil is primarily shallow brashy clay**, overlaying **limestone bedrock**, which drains quickly in drought and compacts easily in wet weather. In one episode, Clarkson lamented how the fields became rock-hard in summer and boot-sucking swamps in winter—an experience any Oxfordshire farmer would nod along to.

Crop choice is a science here, and Clarkson initially tried to play the game by the book: **barley, wheat, and oilseed rape**. These are common staples across Oxfordshire due to their compatibility with the soil and climate. But even these can be risky. Oilseed rape, for instance, has been hit hard in recent years by flea beetle infestations and pesticide bans. Clarkson watched one field wither almost entirely, losing money before the combine ever rolled in.

To diversify, he added **sheep**—perhaps naively. The show captures some of the chaos: escaped lambs, mistaken genders, a never-ending wrestling match with fencing. But sheep make sense here. The Cotswolds have a long pastoral history, and grassland grazing suits the terrain. However, lamb prices fluctuate heavily, and Clarkson quickly learned that the cost of raising animals rarely matches the check you receive come slaughter time.

What makes farming in Oxfordshire doubly difficult is the **land value and surrounding population**. This is not remote Yorkshire or windswept Wales. This is **prime commuter belt territory**, dotted with celebrities, second homes, and conservation-minded councils. That means more bureaucracy, more opposition to development, and more tension between traditional farming and modern expectations.

When Clarkson tried to open a farm shop to sell his produce directly, he ran headfirst into **planning disputes** with West Oxfordshire District Council. What he thought was a simple way to survive turned into a bureaucratic saga. Locals complained about traffic, signage, and noise. The council pushed back. The headlines flared. But behind it all was a serious question: **How can farmers evolve if every step forward meets a red-taped wall?**

The show turned Diddly Squat into a household name, but in reality, it became a **microcosm of national issues**. The idea that owning 1,000 acres of land doesn't guarantee a living struck many viewers as shocking. But for UK farmers, it was all too familiar. Yield doesn't equal profit. You can do everything right and still make nothing. Fertilizer prices rise. Machinery breaks. Crops fail. And the government paperwork never stops.

Clarkson didn't invent these problems—he just filmed them.

And yet, there is something admirable in how he transformed that land into more than just fields and fences. Through trial and error—and a fair amount of embarrassment—he showed how every acre has its own rules. One plot may flood in April but bake dry in June. One hillside may grow wheat beautifully while the next becomes a disaster. Diddly Squat isn't just a farm. It's a character—temperamental, beautiful, stubborn, and full of surprises.

Clarkson's greatest contribution may have been putting real soil back on television—not manicured lawns, but stubborn fields that fight back. His land, like so many across Britain, is unpredictable and unforgiving. But it also holds promise. With the right guidance, investment, and community support, even the most reluctant farmer can bring something from the ground.

And so the name "Diddly Squat," once a joke, became a rallying cry. A reminder that behind every quaint farm gate lies a story of effort, risk, and resilience. Clarkson may have started with nothing. But in revealing the anatomy of his land—its flaws, its promise, and its reality—he gave British farming something more valuable than cash: attention.

Chapter Three

Farming After Brexit – Policy, Panic, and Potential

For decades, UK farming operated within a framework it didn't control but came to depend on—the European Union's Common Agricultural Policy. The CAP wasn't perfect. It rewarded land ownership more than food production and disproportionately favored large estates. But it provided something farmers could rely on: predictability. Then came Brexit, and with it, a slow unraveling of that certainty.

In the years following the 2016 referendum, the British agricultural sector found itself thrust into the unknown. The government promised reforms that would "reward farmers for environmental stewardship" rather than acreage alone, and a new era was announced: one that would prioritize sustainability, biodiversity, and innovation. But as the old payments phased out and the new systems stumbled into implementation, many farmers felt less like they were entering a new era—and more like they were being left behind.

The Environmental Land Management scheme—**ELMs**—was introduced as the crown jewel of the post-Brexit agricultural reform. Under ELMs, farmers would be paid not for how much land they owned, but for what they *did* with it: planting hedgerows, protecting wetlands, rotating crops for soil health. It sounded visionary on paper. In practice, it arrived late, rolled out slowly, and was mired in complexity. By 2022, fewer than one in ten farmers reported having clarity on how to apply or how much they could expect to earn.

One farmer from Wiltshire summed it up in an interview with *The Guardian*: "They've taken away the foundation before building the new house. The old subsidies are gone, and the new ones are either not ready or don't pay enough. It's chaos."

The impact wasn't just financial—it was emotional. For generations, farming in Britain has been shaped by long-term planning, seasonal rhythms, and cautious investments. Suddenly, the ground beneath it felt political, volatile, and short-term. Equipment upgrades were delayed. Hiring plans were shelved. Some considered selling land rather than face years of uncertainty. The trust between farmer and government—already frayed—was now in tatters.

And then came the **labor crisis**.

British farms had long relied on seasonal migrant labor from Eastern Europe—particularly Romania, Bulgaria, and Poland—to harvest fruit, pick vegetables, and tend livestock. Brexit didn't just cut off that labor supply—it replaced it with a visa system too cumbersome for most farms to navigate. The results were devastating. In 2021 alone, over **30,000 tons of crops** reportedly went unharvested due to labor shortages. Some rotted in the fields. Some were plowed under. In Kent, strawberry growers offered bonuses and accommodation, but still couldn't fill the jobs.

Farmers tried to recruit locally, but British workers—many unfamiliar with the stamina and pace required—lasted only days. One Herefordshire farmer told the BBC: "We had people show up late, leave early, and say they were done after lunch. No hard feelings—but this isn't a nine-to-five job. The fruit doesn't wait."

Trade, too, was no longer straightforward. Outside the EU's single market, UK farmers now faced a maze of **export paperwork**, veterinary inspections, and border delays. A cheese producer in Devon, who once sold weekly to customers in France and Germany, watched orders vanish after his shipping costs and customs fees doubled. "They love our products," he said. "But they don't love the new hassle. And neither do I."

In Clarkson's Farm, these complications weren't abstract—they were personal. Scenes where Jeremy sat at his desk, muttering about DEFRA forms or squinting at his farm's finances, became quiet moments of frustration that echoed across rural Britain. The confusion he felt was real. The bureaucracy he wrestled with was not exaggerated. And the questions he asked—"Why does this cost so much?" "Why is this so hard?"—were questions farmers had been asking for years without a camera crew.

And yet, amid the fear and frustration, some farmers began to see opportunity.

The end of CAP meant an end to farming by formula. No longer bound to chase subsidy thresholds, some began exploring

regenerative methods—rotational grazing, cover cropping, rewilding. Others leaned into **direct-to-consumer sales**, using social media, farm shops, and subscription boxes to bypass the middlemen. Diversification became not just smart—but necessary.

Clarkson himself embraced that shift. The **Diddly Squat Farm Shop**, though initially modest, became a national curiosity. It didn't just sell produce—it sold a story. And it reminded farmers that the British public, when shown the human side of agriculture, was willing to support it with their wallets.

Still, optimism was cautious. As of 2023, the government continued to adjust the ELMs scheme in response to criticism. Some regions saw improved pilot programs. Others felt excluded or confused. The NFU continued to press for clearer timelines and fairer payments. Meanwhile, farmers juggled new climate demands, rising fuel costs, and public scrutiny.

Brexit didn't ruin British farming. But it revealed just how fragile its foundations were. It showed how much farmers had come to depend on a system they didn't fully understand until it was gone. And it laid bare a painful truth: that feeding a nation is political, vulnerable, and often thankless work.

Yet in the middle of it all stood farms like Diddly Squat. Loud, messy, imperfect—and deeply real. Through his own missteps, Clarkson captured the mood of a farming nation teetering between tradition and transformation. Brexit, for better or worse, forced UK agriculture to evolve. The question now is: who will survive that evolution, and what will British farming look like when the dust settles?

Chapter Four

The Bureaucratic Battle – Red Tape vs Common Sense

Before he ever planted a seed or sold a potato, Jeremy Clarkson met an opponent far tougher than drought, disease, or diesel costs: bureaucracy. His efforts to run Diddly Squat Farm weren't just challenged by nature—they were frequently strangled by paperwork, planning restrictions, and a slow-churning administrative machine that seems, at times, designed to exhaust rather than assist.

In one memorable episode, Clarkson opens his brand-new farm shop to sell his own produce, only to be met with fierce opposition from the local council. The complaint? Too many cars. Too many people. Too much success. And behind that simple objection lay a deeper issue: the uncomfortable relationship between UK farming and the bureaucracies meant to govern it.

British farmers operate in one of the most highly regulated sectors of the economy. Every step of the agricultural process—from how land is used, to what pesticides can be sprayed, to how eggs are labeled—requires compliance with rules often written by people who've never set foot on a farm. These rules exist for good reason: to protect the environment, public health, and fair trading standards. But when regulation loses touch with practicality, it becomes a trap.

Clarkson's clash with **West Oxfordshire District Council** over signage and parking may have been wrapped in comedy, but it struck a nerve across the country. What started as a man trying to diversify his struggling farm became a months-long battle over planning permission. Neighbors complained about increased traffic. The council responded with restrictions. At one point, Clarkson built a temporary restaurant inside a barn to showcase local food—only to see it shut down under enforcement threats.

To the average viewer, this was entertainment. But to farmers, it was all too real.

Planning permission for even the smallest building—a grain silo, a shed, a shop—requires navigating layers of local authority, environmental impact assessments, and sometimes public consultation. In designated Areas of Outstanding Natural Beauty (AONBs), like much of the Cotswolds, the rules become even stricter. A barn isn't just a barn. It might affect sightlines, traffic flow, or habitat protection. And while those concerns matter, the process to address them often moves at the speed of cold molasses.

Then there's DEFRA—the **Department for Environment, Food and Rural Affairs**—responsible for overseeing the bulk of farming regulation in the UK. DEFRA issues guidance on subsidies, environmental programs, disease control, animal welfare, and everything in between. Its website is a maze. Its forms are infamous. And for small farmers without in-house compliance officers, understanding DEFRA can feel like a full-time job.

Clarkson's on-screen frustration—scrolling through documents, bewildered by grant requirements—echoed a truth many farmers live with daily. Want to plant a hedgerow? There's a form. Want to rotate crops? There's a different form. Want to host a farm tour? That's tourism—better check with another department. Miss a deadline, and your subsidy might be delayed or reduced. Make a clerical error, and the consequences can stretch across seasons.

The history of UK farming regulation traces back over a century. The **Agriculture Act of 1947**, passed after World War II, was a landmark that aimed to secure national food supply and guaranteed prices. Over time, as

Britain joined the EEC (later the EU), layers of European regulation were added—resulting in overlapping systems of control. Even after Brexit, many of these structures remained, slightly rebranded but still burdensome.

In recent years, efforts have been made to simplify things. DEFRA launched online platforms, integrated mapping tools, and streamlined payment schemes. But the core problem remains: the **disconnect between policy and practicality**. Decisions made in London often fail to reflect life on the ground. Clarkson's experience—being told he couldn't sell his own jam because of a missing permit—wasn't an exaggeration. It was a documentary moment that countless farmers recognized instantly.

And the consequences aren't just about inconvenience. Bureaucratic friction discourages innovation. Farmers hesitate to diversify or modernize because of fear: fear of rejection, delays, or penalties. A farmer in Suffolk once explained it simply: "I wanted to open a cider barn. I spent more time filling forms than pressing apples. In the end, I gave up."

Clarkson didn't give up—but he had advantages: money, media attention, and a global audience. Most farmers have none of those things. Their frustrations go unheard, buried under acronyms, phone queues, and department hotlines that promise to help but rarely do.

Still, the show's greatest legacy might be in exposing this silent war. For decades, the image of farming in Britain was romantic: sunsets over hay bales, gumboots and dogs, fresh eggs in wicker baskets. Clarkson ripped the curtain back and revealed what lies beneath: risk, regulation, and relentless red tape.

There are calls now—from the NFU, rural MPs, and even Clarkson himself—for a **common sense approach** to agricultural policy. One that protects the environment without paralyzing progress. One that promotes food security without drowning farmers in documents. Whether those calls will be heard remains uncertain. But one thing is clear: farming isn't just about crops and animals. It's about navigating a bureaucratic system that often feels like it was designed by people with no mud on their boots.

In the fields of Britain today, the greatest harvest may not come from wheat or sheep—but from clarity, flexibility, and finally giving farmers the trust to do the job they already know how to do.

Chapter Five

Risk and Reward – The Harsh Economics of Farming

When Jeremy Clarkson announced that his first year of running Diddly Squat Farm had yielded a profit of just **£144**, many viewers laughed. It seemed absurd that a thousand-acre farm—complete with wheat fields, sheep, and a farm shop—could deliver a return less than a single day's work for most people. But for farmers across Britain, the number wasn't a punchline. It was a painful truth dressed up as comedy.

The economics of farming in the UK are not just tight—they are razor-thin. On paper, farming sounds like a business with guaranteed demand. People need to eat. Land grows food. Add a bit of machinery and labor, and the system should work. But what Clarkson discovered—and what generations of farmers already knew—is that *every step of the process bleeds money before it makes it.*

Let's break it down.

Start with **equipment**. Clarkson's infamous Lamborghini tractor cost around **£40,000**, and that's before fuel, maintenance, and storage. Most farmers don't buy such flashy models, but even a basic second-hand combine harvester can set you back **£75,000–£120,000**, and that's for older tech. Spares are expensive. Repairs are frequent. And if a major machine breaks during harvest, the delay can wipe out your crop's value.

Then there's **seed and fertilizer**. As of 2023, fertilizer costs had skyrocketed due to global supply chain disruptions, with prices doubling in some areas. **Ammonium nitrate**, one of the most common fertilizers, climbed from **£250 per ton to over £700** in less than two years. A farmer planting 100 acres of wheat might spend over **£12,000–£15,000** on fertilizer alone—before the seed even goes into the ground.

Fuel is another recurring expense. Agricultural vehicles run on **red diesel**, which is taxed at a lower rate than road fuel, but the price is still volatile. One full season of field prep, planting, harvesting, and hauling can require thousands of liters, adding **£5,000–£10,000** in fuel costs annually depending on farm size and machinery.

Add **labor**. Even on smaller farms, a solo operator can't do everything. Hiring part-time help for lambing season, harvesting, or machine operation quickly adds up. A skilled tractor driver or shepherd might earn **£10–£15 per hour**, and peak season demands long hours. If a farmer employs two helpers for 10 weeks a year at full-time hours, that's another **£12,000–£15,000** out the door.

Now factor in **livestock**. Sheep, a common choice for grassland farms like Clarkson's, require constant attention. Lambs need vaccines, shelter, mineral supplements, and shearing. Ewes need scanning, feed, and care during birth. One bad winter or parasite outbreak can kill profits. Lamb prices fluctuate wildly, especially when demand dips or supermarkets source cheaper meat from abroad.

And then there's the wildcard: **weather**.

Too much rain floods fields and destroys crops. Not enough rain stunts growth. A late frost can ruin a budding season. No amount of technology can fully protect against these risks. Crop insurance exists, but it doesn't cover every scenario—and the paperwork can be as painful as the loss itself.

In his show, Clarkson openly documented a failed oilseed rape crop, forced replanting, broken fencing from storms, and a few business decisions that probably looked better in theory than execution. But none of that was unusual. It was *familiar*. DEFRA reports show that the average **net farm income for cereal farms** in England between 2021–2023 was around **£46,800**, but that figure includes subsidies—and hides massive variation. Take subsidies away, and many farms fall below **break-even**.

Even with diversification, things don't always improve. The Diddly Squat Farm Shop became a media sensation, with lines of fans hoping to buy "cow juice" and "bee juice." But building the shop, securing permissions, and staffing it brought its own costs. One could argue that the shop made more from Clarkson's fame than from his farming—and for most British farmers, there's no TV deal to lean on.

The **National Farmers' Union (NFU)** has long highlighted these struggles. Their surveys show that 41% of farmers worry about cash flow month-to-month. 50% say they rely on **Basic Payment Scheme** funds to stay afloat. The new Environmental Land Management schemes may one day help—but at present, many farms are losing income faster than they can adapt.

Clarkson's £144 profit was real—but it wasn't rare. Many farmers operate at a loss or break even. They survive on part-time work, family labor, and a belief in the land that defies pure economics. Farming, for them, is not just a business. It's a calling. And increasingly, it's a gamble.

There's a cruel irony in all this: the people who grow our food are often the least rewarded for it. Supermarkets post record profits. Middlemen thrive. But the farmer at the start of the chain faces rising costs, fickle weather, and the relentless squeeze of scale. Clarkson's journey, while colored with humor, revealed that farming isn't just hard work—it's financially perilous.

In a time of rising food prices, cost-of-living crises, and climate uncertainty, understanding the true economics of farming is essential. It isn't enough to admire a picturesque landscape. We have to ask: *What does it take to keep that field growing? Who's paying the price when the harvest fails?* And perhaps most importantly, *how long can farmers keep going if the numbers no longer make sense?*

Chapter Six

Kaleb, Gerald, and the Farming Knowledge Gap

In a show starring one of Britain's loudest celebrities, it was a young man with a country drawl and a fierce love for tractors who quietly stole the spotlight. **Kaleb Cooper**, barely in his twenties when *Clarkson's Farm* began filming, became an instant fan favorite—not for his charm, but for his bluntness. He shouted at Clarkson. He rolled his eyes at mistakes. He mocked the Lambo tractor. And yet, he did it all with the confidence of someone who knows exactly what he's doing.

Kaleb wasn't acting. He's not an influencer. He didn't arrive with a backstory written by producers. He was just a local lad, raised in the Oxfordshire countryside, whose entire life had been built around the land. By the time he met Clarkson, he had more real-world farming experience than his boss—and it showed. While Clarkson fumbled with machinery and grappled with government forms, Kaleb moved through fields with purpose. He didn't just work on the farm. He understood it.

Audiences loved him. His haircut became a meme. His loyalty to the countryside became a rallying cry. But beneath the banter, Kaleb represented something serious: a dwindling generation of young people with practical, inherited agricultural knowledge—and nowhere to grow it.

In many ways, Kaleb is a rare breed. While his fame may seem like a fluke, his background is increasingly uncommon. Fewer and fewer young people in the UK are entering farming, not because they lack interest, but because they lack access. **Farming apprenticeships** have declined, agricultural colleges are underfunded, and land ownership remains out of reach for most. Add to that the pressure to leave rural areas for better-paid urban jobs, and the result is a growing **skills gap** in one of the nation's oldest professions.

The **Office for National Statistics** reports that the average age of a UK farmer is now **59 years old**. Over half are over 60. Meanwhile, the number of full-time under-25s working in agriculture has dropped by nearly 40% in the last two decades. It's not that the youth are lazy—it's that farming, in its current economic and social structure, offers fewer clear paths for them to succeed.

Kaleb, in his stubborn refusal to leave the countryside, became an unintentional symbol of resistance. He famously declared that he'd never been to London and had no interest in ever going. That line made people laugh—but it also resonated. Here was a young man proudly rooted in a place the rest of the world often overlooks. He knew the land, its moods, and its needs better than any spreadsheet ever could.

Then there's **Gerald Cooper**, Clarkson's softly spoken stone wall specialist with a thick Gloucestershire accent and decades of experience in rural trades. Gerald, often unintelligible even to subtitles, became a cult hero of his own. While younger viewers struggled to understand his words, farmers and rural Brits heard every sentence clearly. Gerald represented a kind of old-world wisdom that's slowly disappearing—knowledge not from textbooks, but from generations of doing.

He didn't explain soil health. He showed it in the way he planted hedges and repaired dry stone walls. His expertise wasn't flashy. It was felt. When he walked a fence line or gestured toward a field, he did so with the quiet authority of someone who had watched that land for 40 years.

Together, Kaleb and Gerald bookend the spectrum of agricultural knowledge. One young, passionate, and frustrated by limitations. The other seasoned, humble, and rarely heard in public conversations. Both exposed something Clarkson's fame helped amplify: **the most valuable knowledge in farming isn't digital—it's lived**.

Unfortunately, lived knowledge is vulnerable. As older generations retire, there's no guarantee their wisdom passes on. Too many farms close without successors. Too few young people stay in agriculture long enough to absorb the nuances. And formal education systems often lag behind the practical needs of modern farming. While tech and agri-science are promoted, hands-on skills—like repairing fencing, managing livestock, or reading weather patterns—are disappearing.

In recent years, organizations like the **Prince's Countryside Fund** and the **Landworkers' Alliance** have pushed for reforms. They call for new training programs, easier access to land, and better pathways for young entrants. But progress is slow, and the gap continues to grow.

Kaleb's rise to fame did something extraordinary. It made **competence cool**. For once, a young man who could reverse a trailer, balance seed inputs, and predict a rainstorm by instinct wasn't background noise—he was the main story. His success gave voice to thousands of unseen rural workers who've kept farms running without applause. And it forced city-based audiences to realize that **knowing how to grow food is not a lesser form of intelligence—it's survival knowledge**.

Clarkson may have owned the land, but Kaleb and Gerald *understood* it. They didn't just operate machinery—they respected the rhythms of nature. Their inclusion in the show wasn't just comic relief. It was education. And perhaps more importantly, it was a call to action.

If Britain is to secure the future of its farms, it must invest not just in technology, but in **people**—the ones with muddy boots, weathered hands, and eyes that can read a field like a map. Because when those people retire, and no one's there to take their place, no app or drone will be able to fix what we've lost.

Chapter Seven

Farming and Climate – Droughts, Floods, and Emissions

In one episode of *Clarkson's Farm*, Jeremy gazes across a soaked field and mutters something every British farmer has likely said: "It's either too wet or too dry—never just right." That offhand comment, thrown out for laughs, cuts straight to the heart of a crisis reshaping UK agriculture from the soil up.

For generations, farmers have dealt with unpredictable weather. But in recent years, the weather hasn't just been unpredictable—it's become extreme. Fields that once handled rain now flood. Summers that once nurtured crops now bake them into the earth. **Climate change**, long dismissed as a future threat, is now an everyday, tangible force that shapes every planting schedule, every harvest, and every risk calculation.

In 2018, parts of the UK experienced one of the most severe **droughts** in modern memory. River levels dropped, irrigation bans were issued, and yields fell. Farmers across the southeast reported crop losses of up to **40%**, particularly in cereals and root vegetables. Then, in a whiplash reversal, the winter of 2019–2020 brought record-breaking **flooding**, submerging thousands of hectares and delaying spring planting. Each year since has delivered more of the same: erratic patterns, reduced predictability, and mounting pressure.

These aren't isolated events. The **Met Office and UK Climate Projections (UKCP18)** warn that the country will see warmer, wetter winters and hotter, drier summers by 2050—conditions that threaten the very viability of traditional crops. Wheat, the backbone of many arable farms, becomes risky without proper moisture. Oilseed rape is already suffering under pest pressures worsened by mild winters. Livestock farmers, too, face challenges: heat stress in animals, unreliable grazing pastures, and water shortages.

Meanwhile, farmers aren't just victims of climate change—they're being asked to become its **frontline fighters**. Agriculture in the UK accounts for approximately **10% of national greenhouse gas emissions**, with most coming from methane (via livestock), nitrous oxide (via fertilizers), and carbon dioxide (via machinery and soil disturbance). The government has made it clear: emissions must fall, and the countryside must play its part.

But how?

Some of the pressure comes with support. The **Environmental Land Management schemes (ELMs)** introduced post-Brexit now offer payments for practices that protect or restore nature: planting hedgerows, improving soil health, creating pollinator habitats, and reducing fertilizer use. For example, a farmer who switches to **no-till farming**—a method that avoids ploughing and thus keeps carbon locked in the soil—can qualify for financial incentives.

Others are turning to **precision farming**. GPS-guided tractors and drone surveys help apply exactly the right amount of seed, pesticide, or fertilizer—reducing waste and emissions. Sensors monitor soil moisture in real time. Apps track livestock movement and health, minimizing unnecessary inputs. These tools don't just improve efficiency—they make farming more climate-resilient.

Then there are **grassroots innovations**, born not from policy but from desperation and ingenuity. In Yorkshire, a collective of dairy farmers began **rotational grazing**, moving cattle frequently to mimic natural patterns and regenerate soil. In Cornwall, some growers replaced chemical sprays with **biological pest controls** like ladybird colonies and pheromone traps. In Wales, young shepherds turned to **mobile milking parlors** powered by solar panels, reaching remote flocks without burning diesel.

These stories don't always make the news, but they matter. They show a shift in thinking—not just about yield, but about legacy. Farmers are no longer managing fields for this season alone. They're asking: *What will this land look like in thirty years? What will my children inherit?*

Yet, the road is far from smooth. Adoption of sustainable methods often requires **capital investment**, and margins remain tight. Some schemes are difficult to understand or access. And while climate action is framed as urgent, policy rollout is often slow. As one farmer told *The Times*, "They want me to plant trees, but won't tell me which kind, or where, or how to apply. Meanwhile, my fence just washed away again."

Clarkson's show didn't dwell heavily on climate change, but it hinted at its impact. Flooded tracks, destroyed crops, and failed field plans told their own story. He learned, as many do, that the land no longer obeys old rhythms. Farming, once a dance with the seasons, has become a battle against instability.

But in that battle, there is opportunity.

The same land that can sequester carbon also feeds the nation. The same hedgerow that shelters wildlife also buffers floodwaters. British farms can become climate heroes—not just victims—if given the tools, the time, and the trust.

The climate is changing. The question isn't whether farmers will respond. It's whether the country will support them in doing so—before the window closes, and the fields fall silent not from drought or flood, but from abandonment.

Chapter Eight

Mental Health and Isolation on the Farm

There's a moment in *Clarkson's Farm* when Jeremy, standing in a cold, empty field after another setback, mutters to no one in particular: "It's just me and the mud." It's played for dry humor, but the line lingers. Because behind the muddy boots, machinery, and sheep chaos lies something much quieter—and much more serious. For thousands of farmers across the UK, *it really is just them and the mud*. Day after day. Week after week.

Farming, by its nature, is an isolating profession. Long hours, remote locations, financial strain, and emotional burden make it one of the loneliest jobs in the country.

There are no colleagues at the next desk. No 9-to-5 clock-off. And no guarantee that the year's work will pay off. When the crops fail or the animals fall ill, the farmer often faces it alone—with no safety net but their own grit.

In 2022, the **Office for National Statistics** reported that **suicide rates among male agricultural workers were among the highest of any occupation in the UK**. Charities like **RABI (The Royal Agricultural Benevolent Institution)** and **The Farming Community Network (FCN)** have long sounded the alarm: farmers are silently suffering. A 2021 survey conducted by RABI found that **36% of farmers in England and Wales described themselves as "probably" or "possibly" depressed,** while nearly half had experienced anxiety in the past year.

What makes this crisis harder to address is that it's often invisible. Farmers are known for their stoicism. Generations of working through adversity have created a culture of self-reliance—one that sometimes confuses strength with silence. Many don't talk. Many don't ask for help. And far too many don't realize they're struggling until it's too late.

Clarkson's Farm brought unexpected visibility to this crisis—not through direct messaging, but through its tone and structure. The series wasn't just about tractors and yields; it was about stress. About trying to do something meaningful and failing. About dealing with rules you don't understand, weather you can't control, and critics who don't care. Scenes of Jeremy alone in his kitchen, calculating losses, or pacing a field after another plan collapses, carried a quiet emotional weight. It was entertainment, yes. But for many farmers watching, it was also *recognition*.

The rural mental health crisis has many roots.

Financial instability is a constant. With margins thin, debt rising, and subsidies uncertain, even the most productive farms can fall into the red. When income depends on forces outside your control—markets, weather, policy—stress becomes chronic. Add in **bureaucracy**, and even the most resilient farmers are worn down. Farmers often spend more time filling out forms than tending their crops. The psychological toll of uncertainty is real.

Then there's **physical isolation**. Unlike urban jobs, where co-workers provide daily social interaction, many farmers spend hours—sometimes days—without speaking to anyone but their animals. During the pandemic, this intensified. Livestock auctions were suspended. Social gatherings halted. Community events, already dwindling in rural Britain, vanished entirely. For older farmers, especially those living alone, the result was a profound sense of being forgotten.

Charities have stepped up. RABI now offers **confidential mental health counseling**, online therapy, and peer support networks. FCN runs a **24/7 helpline**, staffed by volunteers with farming backgrounds. In Scotland, the **RSABI** has begun integrating mental health checks into financial support calls. These groups don't just hand out advice—they listen, often becoming the first human voice a struggling farmer has heard in days.

Stories abound. A dairy farmer in Shropshire, overwhelmed by debt and the death of a parent, credits a single phone call to RABI with saving his life. A young tenant farmer in Cornwall admitted in an interview: "The hardest part wasn't the work. It was the silence. The sense that if I disappeared, no one would notice for weeks."

Government awareness is growing, but slowly. In 2023, DEFRA launched a campaign to support mental health in farming, emphasizing stigma reduction and better access to services. But challenges remain: funding is thin, rural mental health providers are scarce, and broadband access—crucial for online counseling—is still unreliable in many areas.

Clarkson himself addressed the topic indirectly. In interviews, he described farming as "the hardest thing I've ever done," and not just physically. He spoke of feeling stupid, helpless, and alone when the numbers didn't add up or when the animals died. His visibility brought these feelings into the mainstream. If a celebrity known for confidence could admit to struggling, maybe other farmers could, too.

The truth is, fields don't just grow crops. They grow pressure. The expectation to carry on, to maintain family legacy, to feed a nation—all without complaint—creates a quiet, internal storm that's hard to spot until it breaks.

Farming doesn't need heroes. It needs help. Community. Connection. A system that sees the human being behind the produce sticker. And a culture that understands that asking for support isn't weakness—it's wisdom.

As the spotlight on British farming continues to grow, so must our empathy. Not just for the challenges we can see—the floods, the failed crops, the finances—but for the ones we can't. Because the most dangerous thing in a field isn't always a storm. Sometimes, it's silence.

Chapter Nine

Farm Shops and Local Economies – Rebuilding from the Ground Up

It began as a shed at the edge of a field. A bit of signage, some homegrown potatoes, and a fridge full of unpasteurized milk. But soon, **Diddly Squat Farm Shop** became one of the most talked-about destinations in the Cotswolds. What started as Jeremy Clarkson's personal project to sell produce from his struggling farm exploded into a phenomenon that had traffic queues winding down country lanes, cameras flashing beside hay bales, and social media buzzing with photos of "cow juice" and "bee juice."

But behind the clever branding and celebrity halo was something deeply instructive: a live experiment in what happens when farmers sell directly to the people who eat their food. And, perhaps more importantly, what happens to a rural economy when a farm becomes more than just a field.

Farm shops aren't new. For decades, they've served as modest outlets for surplus eggs, vegetables, and jars of jam. But in the last 10–15 years, they've evolved into something more ambitious—a **movement**. One that reconnects consumers with the origin of their food, cuts out intermediaries, and gives farmers a chance to survive without relying solely on commodity markets.

Clarkson's version of the farm shop pushed that model into public consciousness. At Diddly Squat, the products were hyper-local and proudly unpolished. The shelves weren't lined with polished branding, but with goods that felt authentic—messy vegetables, raw milk, and artisanal honey. The shop celebrated the flaws. It made "realness" the selling point. And customers didn't just buy—they posted. They shared. They queued. They turned up in droves, spending not just money, but attention.

For struggling farms across the UK, it was a revelation.

Farm-to-table culture, once considered niche or urban, is now a growing economic lifeline. The rise of localism—accelerated by the pandemic and by Brexit supply chain challenges—has led more Britons to ask where their food comes from. They want to know the farmer's name. They want to support someone they can see. And they're often willing to pay a little more for that connection.

For farmers, this shift has opened doors. A bag of potatoes sold to a supermarket might bring in 20p per kilo. Sold at a farm shop? That same bag might fetch £2—plus a conversation, plus a returning customer. Add in baked goods, preserves, pick-your-own fruit, or seasonal events, and suddenly, a farm is no longer just a producer—it's a destination.

These changes ripple outward. When a farm shop thrives, so does the village butcher, the local bakery, the nearby B&B. Tourism follows. So do jobs. So does pride.

In 2021, the **Farm Retail Association** reported a surge in interest from farmers wanting to open or expand farm shops, with

83% saying their turnover had increased during the COVID era. Many credited not just consumer demand, but the sense of **community resilience** that local food systems provide. In tough times, people turned not to big chains, but to each other.

Diddly Squat proved how powerful that pull could be—but it also showed the challenges. The influx of visitors to Clarkson's farm caused traffic chaos. Local councils clamped down. Neighbors complained. Suddenly, the same success that revitalized one piece of farmland threatened to overwhelm the village. And therein lies the tension at the heart of modern rural commerce: *How do you grow without losing what made you valuable in the first place?*

For smaller farms, the answer lies in balance. Farm shops don't have to become theme parks. Many succeed quietly—offering eggs at the gate, hosting weekend markets, or collaborating with other local artisans. Some launch **community-supported agriculture (CSA)** schemes, where residents pay upfront for a share of the harvest. Others run school tours, seasonal fairs, or on-site cafés. The key isn't scale—it's authenticity.

Social media has also played a critical role. Farmers like Kaleb Cooper now use Instagram and TikTok to share the rhythms of daily life—feeding calves, fixing machinery, or cracking jokes in the rain. These snippets humanize farming. They turn "producers" into personalities. And in doing so, they drive sales, visits, and advocacy.

Clarkson, intentionally or not, built a template: combine storytelling with sustainability. Create a product that is not just edible, but **experience-driven**. Invite people into the process. Let them walk the field, pet the lamb, and buy a bag of spuds from the person who dug them up. In an age of mass production and anonymous supply chains, that intimacy is rare—and valuable.

Not every farm can pull off what Diddly Squat did. Fame is a megaphone few possess. But the principle applies widely: when farmers reclaim their place in the market—not as cogs, but as curators—they gain power. And when communities support them, they gain something even more important: **resilience**.

The future of British farming may not lie in supermarkets, but in lay-bys and village lanes. In handmade signs, in jam jars with handwritten labels, in conversations at the counter. Farm shops aren't just about selling food. They're about **rooting economies in the land again**, one transaction—and one relationship—at a time.

Chapter Ten

Agricultural Innovation – The Future is (Finally) Now

At first glance, farming and technology seem like opposites—one rooted in ancient rhythms, the other born from rapid change. But in the fields of modern Britain, the plough is giving way to precision lasers, and the shepherd's whistle is being replaced by data pings from wearable sensors. The future of agriculture isn't just coming. It's already here. And for many farmers, it couldn't have arrived fast enough.

As Jeremy Clarkson wrestled with broken fences, stubborn sheep, and weather-wrecked fields, viewers saw just how hard traditional farming could be. But *Clarkson's Farm* also hinted at a bigger question: *Is there a better way to farm?* Not easier—but smarter, faster, more efficient? Across the UK, a growing number of farmers are answering that question with action. They're trading guesswork for algorithms, muscle for microchips, and instinct for insight.

Take **GPS-guided tractors**, for example. Once reserved for mega-farms in the American Midwest, they're now appearing across Britain. These machines can drive in straight lines accurate to within two centimeters, reducing soil compaction, eliminating overlap, and saving fuel. Clarkson himself marveled at the feature—though he quickly admitted the controls were beyond him. In skilled hands, however, GPS systems slash operating costs and environmental impact in equal measure.

Even more futuristic are the **drones** hovering over British fields. Lightweight and agile, these flying assistants capture high-resolution imagery that detects crop health, pest infestations, or nutrient deficiencies days before they're visible to the human eye. In Cambridgeshire, one arable farmer uses drone data to create variable rate maps—telling his sprayers exactly where to apply and where to skip. The result? He cut pesticide use by 20% and improved yields in poor-performing zones.

Then there's the **data revolution in livestock care**. On a dairy farm in Somerset, every cow wears a collar that tracks movement, rumination, and temperature in real time. If a cow eats less, limps, or shows signs of illness, the system sends an alert to the farmer's phone. Early detection means faster treatment, better welfare, and lower veterinary costs. No more relying on visual checks alone. The animals themselves now "talk" to the farmer—digitally.

In **Yorkshire**, sheep farmers are using **electronic identification (EID) tags** not just for traceability, but to build performance databases. Each ewe's reproductive success, weight gain of lambs, and response to treatment are logged and analyzed. Decisions once made by gut feeling—culling, breeding, feeding—are now driven by evidence. These are not just efficiencies. They are *survival strategies* in an industry where margins are measured in pennies per kilo.

The rise of **Artificial Intelligence** is the next frontier. AI programs, trained on years of weather, yield, and soil data, can now recommend the optimal planting time for each crop in a field—adjusting daily forecasts and historical performance. In Kent, a fruit grower tested an AI-powered orchard management system that reduced labor hours by 30% and minimized water use by nearly half.

Government support is slowly catching up. Through DEFRA's **Farming Innovation Programme**, grants are now available for projects exploring robotics, autonomous machinery, and advanced breeding technologies. One flagship case: the **Hands-Free Hectare** project at Harper Adams University, where researchers managed to grow, monitor, and harvest an entire crop without human hands ever touching the soil. Machines planted the seeds. Drones monitored progress. Driverless combines did the cutting. It sounds like science fiction, but it's already been done—twice.

Still, innovation isn't always about high-tech. Sometimes, it's about **rethinking systems**. In Devon, a cooperative of small-scale farms now shares machinery via a booking app, reducing the cost barrier of buying big equipment. In Wales, a solar-powered vertical farm inside a shipping container grows herbs and salad year-round, immune to weather and using 90% less water. And on the outskirts of Manchester, a regenerative farm uses compost tea and cover crops instead of synthetic fertilizers—producing higher nutrient density and healthier soil.

The challenge isn't whether the tools exist—it's **access**. Many small and mid-size farms can't afford the upfront costs of advanced tech. Others lack the training or broadband speed to use it. And some, understandably, are skeptical. After all, these are livelihoods on the line. A glitchy app could mean a failed harvest. A broken drone doesn't milk a cow.

But the trend is clear: **agriculture is changing**, not just in boardrooms and research labs, but in hedged fields and barnyards. Clarkson's experience with his oversized tractor and his battles with weather reminded viewers of how hard the old way can be. The new way doesn't promise ease—but it does offer options.

What these innovations bring—whether it's a satellite map or a sensor in a hoof—is *time*. Time to plan instead of react. Time to fix the root of a problem, not just the symptoms. And time, perhaps, to enjoy the job again, knowing that the land is working with you, not against you.

In the end, the British farmer of tomorrow may not wear a lab coat or code in Python—but they *will* use a screen as much as a spade. The fields will still need feet. But those feet might just be guided by drones, informed by algorithms, and supported by a new kind of knowledge—one where ancient instincts meet artificial intelligence. And where the future of farming finally begins to feel not like a threat, but a tool in hand.

Chapter Eleven

Media, Myth, and Modernity – The Role of Storytelling in Farming

For most people in Britain, daily contact with farming is rare. They live in cities. They work in offices. They shop in supermarkets. They see milk in bottles and vegetables in plastic—but rarely the hand that milked the cow or tilled the soil. And yet, the idea of "the countryside" remains deeply embedded in British culture—thanks, largely, to **storytelling**.

Whether through radio waves, books, or television screens, media has long painted a picture of rural life. Sometimes it's idyllic and sun-drenched, filled with hay bales and hearty breakfasts. Other times it's grim, muddy, and marked by tragedy. But in nearly every case, **media shapes what the urban majority believes farming to be**—and that belief affects everything from policy to empathy to the price of produce.

One of the earliest—and most enduring—examples is **The Archers**, the BBC's long-running radio soap opera. Launched in 1951 as a public information tool to promote modern farming techniques after World War II, it quickly evolved into a national institution. For many listeners, it was (and remains) their only consistent window into the agricultural world. It taught audiences about foot-and-mouth disease, crop subsidies, and generational farm drama—all through fictional characters in the fictional village of Ambridge.

But The Archers, like many portrayals, was always a blend of realism and comfort. It walked a line between the educational and the entertaining, never veering too far into the truly bleak realities of farming—bankruptcies, suicides, or policy breakdowns. It showed hardship, but it also offered hope. And for that reason, it became a cultural security blanket for rural Britain, reinforcing the idea that, no matter what, the village would carry on.

Fast-forward to 2021, and another voice entered the agricultural conversation—**Jeremy Clarkson**, shouting from atop a hill in Oxfordshire. *Clarkson's Farm* did what few shows ever dared: it made farming messy. It made it frustrating. And most importantly, it made it funny. Viewers didn't just learn about yield per hectare—they saw the emotional toll of failure. They saw a man famous for fast cars and loud opinions humbled by sheep, rain, and bureaucracy.

Media analysts were quick to take note. Dr. Hannah Davis, a cultural sociologist at the University of Sussex, called *Clarkson's Farm* "a watershed moment in public engagement with agriculture." In an interview, she noted: "For the first time in a generation, people were watching farming not as a backdrop to a romance or a murder mystery—but as the main event. And they were loving it."

The success of the show wasn't just in the story—it was in the *shift*. Suddenly, farming wasn't quaint. It was chaotic. And real. Clarkson's failures created empathy. His questions mirrored those of a clueless public. Why is fertiliser so expensive? Why can't I build a shed? Why is the system so complex? In answering those questions, the show taught more about British agriculture in eight episodes than some textbooks do in a year.

But Clarkson didn't do it alone. He followed a legacy of rural representation that includes everything from *Countryfile*—the BBC's flagship farming and countryside program—to *This Farming Life*, a documentary series that captures the quiet dignity of real farmers across Scotland and Northern England. Each of these shows adds a different note to the national melody. *Countryfile* is polished and informative. *This Farming Life* is intimate and unfiltered.

Clarkson's Farm is loud, chaotic, and unexpectedly touching.

What they all share is the power to **shape perception**. And that perception matters.

When viewers believe that farming is easy, they resent rising food prices. When they think all farmers are wealthy landowners, they dismiss subsidy support. But when they see a man crying over a failed lambing season, or a young farmworker struggling with bureaucracy, they begin to understand. And understanding breeds respect.

Sociologists often describe this as the "rural imaginary"—the collection of ideas, myths, and assumptions that urban dwellers carry about the countryside. For decades, that imaginary was defined by heritage tourism ads, BBC dramas, and pastoral poetry. It created affection—but also distortion. It made the countryside feel timeless, unchanging, and safe. But real farming is none of those things.

Clarkson's Farm cracked that illusion. It showed farming as it really is: unpredictable, exhausting, deeply entangled with regulation, and yet—despite all of that—*worth doing.*

And the show's reach didn't end at national borders. It found audiences worldwide, many of whom had never seen British agriculture up close. Viewers from the U.S., Australia, and beyond wrote in to say they finally understood why their own farmers were protesting, struggling, or leaving the land.

This isn't to say that every media portrayal needs to be gritty or painful. There is still space for beauty, nostalgia, and tradition. But the more accurate our media becomes, the more likely our policy will follow. The more realistic the story, the more informed the public. And that, in turn, can change the course of farming's future.

Because stories don't just reflect reality—they *shape* it. And in a time when the future of farming is uncertain, the story we choose to tell about it might be our most important crop of all.

Chapter Twelve

Lessons from Diddly Squat – For Viewers and Farmers Alike

When *Clarkson's Farm* first aired, no one could have predicted the ripple effect it would cause. What began as a celebrity sideshow transformed into a surprisingly raw, unfiltered look at modern farming—and sparked one of the most impactful national conversations about agriculture in decades. But now, several seasons in, it's worth asking: *What exactly did the show teach us? And what did it leave out?*

For many viewers, the show was their first real exposure to the **realities of farming**. They saw not just tractors and lambs, but spreadsheets, red tape, long days, and financial stress. Clarkson's frustrations became a kind of proxy for every confused landowner trying to navigate environmental restrictions, planning permission, or DEFRA's endless forms. In that sense, the series was more than entertaining—it was educational.

Critics, farmers, and policy analysts alike have praised the show for putting a face to the invisible. As rural sociologist **Dr. Emma James** notes, "Clarkson may have arrived at farming as a beginner, but he became a translator—making the invisible bureaucracy and hardship visible to an audience that had no idea what lay behind their Sunday roast." The show gave the general public something they rarely get: *empathy for the people who feed them.*

The most significant **lesson from Diddly Squat** was that farming is not just physical labor—it's constant decision-making under pressure. Should I plant wheat this year or try barley? Can I afford new fencing? Should I hire help, or do it myself? Every choice has financial and environmental consequences. And, as Clarkson learned, even a single misstep—a missed invoice, a botched sheep shearing—can derail an entire season's work.

The series also highlighted the **absurdities of bureaucracy**. Viewers saw Clarkson's attempts to build a farm shop blocked by planning committees. They watched him navigate complex regulations around signage, parking, and product labeling. These weren't exaggerations. Farmers across the UK recognized their own headaches in his complaints. The show turned the faceless nature of regulation into a shared frustration—and in doing so, made it feel urgent.

And then there was the **human element**. Kaleb Cooper and Gerald weren't just sidekicks—they became symbols of knowledge passed through generations. Kaleb's deep-rooted connection to the land, and his no-nonsense attitude, reminded viewers that competence doesn't always come with a degree. Gerald's quiet presence offered dignity to the kind of rural workers so often ignored. These men represented thousands like them across the UK—skilled, experienced, and underappreciated.

But for all its honesty, the show wasn't perfect.

Some **critics argue** that *Clarkson's Farm* still oversimplified parts of the agricultural landscape. The focus on one large, privately-owned farm doesn't reflect the pressures faced by **tenant farmers**, who don't own their land and often operate under stricter financial and legal constraints. Likewise, Clarkson's celebrity status—while used effectively—granted him privileges other farmers do not have. He could afford mistakes, recover from losses, and attract visitors in numbers most rural businesses could only dream of.

Others pointed out that the show, while emotionally honest, sometimes downplayed the **mental health crisis** in farming. Yes, stress and frustration were shown, but the deeper, quieter realities—loneliness, suicide risk, generational pressure—were touched on only briefly. For a profession facing some of the highest suicide rates in the UK, that omission felt like a missed opportunity.

Some **policy experts** also criticized the series for not fully addressing the **diversity** of UK farming. The industry isn't just white men in wellies. There are female farmers, migrant workers, tenant operators, and urban growers. The lens of the show was narrow, centered on one man's journey. Valuable as that was, it didn't reflect the full picture.

Still, the impact is undeniable. DEFRA staff reported a noticeable uptick in public inquiries about farming support and environmental schemes after the show's release. Agricultural colleges noted a rise in applications. And perhaps most tellingly, everyday conversations about land, food, and farming became more curious, more informed, and more compassionate.

In the words of **NFU President Minette Batters**, "Clarkson may not be the perfect farmer, but he created the perfect storm. He brought our struggles into the light—warts and all—and made them visible to people who'd never thought about where food comes from."

The lesson, then, is twofold.

For viewers, *Clarkson's Farm* was a crash course in rural reality. It taught that farming isn't quaint—it's complex. It isn't always profitable. And it rarely goes to plan. It showed that behind every bottle of milk or loaf of bread is someone who got up early, gambled on the weather, and navigated a wall of paperwork just to make it happen.

For farmers, it was a reminder of their value—and their visibility. The show proved that their work is interesting, important, and worthy of national attention. It showed that people *do* care—when given a story they can connect to.

In the end, Diddly Squat was more than a farm. It was a stage, and Clarkson—accidental farmer, bumbling boss, and unlikely advocate—used that stage to tell a story the country didn't know it needed to hear. It wasn't perfect. But it was real. And sometimes, that's the best place to start.

Sowing Seeds of Understanding

No one expected it to matter. When Jeremy Clarkson decided to turn the cameras on his farm in the Cotswolds, most assumed the result would be comic chaos—something to laugh at between replays of *The Grand Tour*. But what emerged was something richer. Something that slipped past the jokes and tractors and straight into the national conversation: a long-overdue recognition of the people who put food on our tables.

Clarkson's Farm did what generations of rural communities have struggled to do—it made farming visible. Not just the rolling hills and picturesque sunsets, but the worry, the work, the waiting. It turned DEFRA forms into story arcs and soil health into suspense. Most of all, it invited the public to care. And they did.

That care matters. For too long, the gulf between cities and fields has grown wider. Fewer people than ever know someone who farms. Fewer children learn where their food comes from. But for a brief moment, one unlikely show pulled that conversation back into living rooms, pubs, classrooms, and headlines. And in doing so, it reminded us of something essential: that farming is not an old-fashioned trade. It is the foundation of every modern life.

The sympathy the show generated wasn't about Clarkson. It was about **recognition**. In Kaleb's frustration, viewers saw the frustration of young people shut out of opportunity. In Gerald's quiet dignity, they saw the wisdom of a generation that rarely gets asked to speak. And in Clarkson's failures, they saw the truth: this work is hard, and the systems designed to support it often don't.

But a show is just a beginning. If the momentum ends when the credits roll, the opportunity is wasted. That's why we must keep farming in the spotlight—*not because it's glamorous, but because it's invisible until it's not.*

Policymakers must act not just with consultation, but with immersion. Let them spend a day on a small family farm, not just review a policy brief. Let them walk the length of a field and try to explain planning permission to a weather-beaten fence post.

Agricultural policy should not be written in offices—it should be informed by the land.

Schools must reintroduce the countryside into the curriculum—not as nostalgia, but as science, economy, and sustainability. Children should understand soil like they understand screen time. They should know how milk is produced, not just how it's packaged. Whether through school garden programs, farm visits, or digital tours, we can make food literacy as essential as math or reading.

Communities, too, have a role. Buy from farm shops when you can. Support local producers. Volunteer during harvest festivals or open farm days. Celebrate the land not just with postcards, but with participation. Rural Britain is not just a tourist attraction—it's a living, breathing part of our national identity.

And finally, the **media** must continue to tell these stories. Clarkson opened the door, but others must walk through it. There are women running dairy farms solo. Migrant workers who make harvests possible. Black and Asian British farmers reclaiming space in a whitewashed industry. There are thousands of untold stories that deserve screen time, microphone time, and page space.

If we want a future where food is secure, land is protected, and rural communities thrive, then farming must remain part of the national imagination. Not just during crises. Not just during TV seasons. But always.

Because the truth is simple: *without farmers, there is no future.* And the seeds of understanding that were planted by Diddly Squat—awkward, muddy, hopeful—will only grow if we keep tending them.

Printed in Dunstable, United Kingdom

70291514R00067